Eggs to Ashes

Practical Tips, Tools and Techniques
for Loving, Grieving, Dreaming & Healing

Mario Lorenzo

Copyright © 2020 Mario Lorenzo

No part of this publication may be reproduced or transmitted
in any manner without the author's written permission
except in the case of brief quotations contained
in critical articles or reviews.

**The front cover mask is the Universal Human.
The bottom half is the conscious part of us
and includes all flesh colors; the top half
is the unconscious creative and hidden self.**

**The back cover mask is the Rainbow Creative Clown
that symbolizes your transformative soul.**

ISBN: 979-8-6948-8865-3

Table of Contents

Preface and Thanks	3
Chapter One: Early Beginnings	5
Chapter Two: Right-Brain Person Living in a Left-Brain World	13
Chapter Three: All Therapy is Grief Therapy	37
Chapter Four: How to Massage a Dream	59
Chapter Five: Wholistic Health	75
Chapter Six: Relationship is Life	87
Chapter Seven: Discoveries Along My Mississippi Cruise	101
Other Resources	107

*To My Parents
Lena and Mario*

*and my sisters
Doris and Diann*

Eggs to Ashes

Practical Tips, Tools and Techniques
for Loving, Grieving, Dreaming & Healing

Preface and Thanks

I started this Practical Guide with the purpose of assisting others with the Global Climate Crisis and the Global Pandemic Covid Virus intervened. Both challenges utilize similar practical tips, tools and techniques for striving, thriving, and surviving. I wish you well in all three areas staying safe, sane, secure, and serene no matter what life offers you.

This dream legacy and destiny is two years evolving. "Take what you want and leave the rest." We are all ONE!

So, skip to the Chapters that interest you and enjoy the Buffet presented. Dig deep and be rewarded.

My grateful thanks to my Ghostwriter Jan Henrikson, my Publisher Richard Fenwick, my reader/editor Dr. Michael Lipparelli, PhD, and Peter Woods, JD, MA, LPC, my computer whiz Steve Adger and Computer assistant Mohamed Omar Makram, CPA, along with many persons who collaborated, instructed, educated, informed and shared along my life's' journey. Cheers and Blessings.

Chapter One

Early Beginnings

I was born two months after the Pearl Harbor attack to Italian parents—the only son—on my father's birthday. I had two sisters, one thirteen years older, one three years younger. I experienced subtle bigotry and racism in my life.

In the four stages of family birth order, there's the hero, the scapegoat, the lonely child, and the mascot or clown. Since there was a large age difference, my older sister thought she was the hero. But when I appeared, I was the superhero, the white crow.

My older sister 13 years older got married by the time

Me at four years old in hat, red sweater and white pants

I was five. Born in a small town of about 5,000 people in Northeastern Nevada, my dad was owner of a small grocery store, where we all worked together. So, my life centered around school, working in my dad's store, play and church.

Being Italian, I was a Tribal Catholic. My life was like living in a sheltered womb. I was born at the start of World War II and then in 1945... there's a picture of me at 4 years old. My mother dressed me up. There was rationing and suffering. In 1946, on my birthday, she took this picture. I remember it because I never wore a hat and white pants because I'd get them dirty in ten seconds. I had an uneventful life—it was store, church, play, and school.

Then when I was 14—my parents disliked public high school, but they believed I could become whatever I wanted to be with a great education. There's no limits. I understood that they wanted me to go to a boarding school. I thought, I like to serve people.

I learned service by serving customers in the grocery store from the age of 7 to 16, as an altar boy in church, in the Boy Scouts earning merit badges and camping out. My town was endowed with adult veterans who served their Country, got the G.I. Bill, graduated, and gave back to the community paying it forward in dedication and service.

I still remember one profound story. I was with my Dad in the store and a lady entered carrying a frozen cherry pie with a wooden knot in it. She said she had bought it from our store and requested her money back, which my Dad did. After she left, I told my Dad did he notice the wrapping around the pie, because it was a brand from a chain store! He said, "The customer is always right!" It's service with a smile.

As a summer flagman working for the State Highway Department assisting tourists during highway maintenance, or as a summer Employment Interviewer for the State Employment Office providing ranchers with hay hands was all about service. Living above the store we were always ready to serve customers and my Dad always fed homeless persons who came begging because of his poor Italian childhood.

"Give and you shall receive," he said. We prayed the Rosary every night at home for "the family that prays together, stays together."

I thought—well, there's doctors, lawyers, bartenders, and laborers. I was an altar boy. I was very close to the church. I admired the behavior of the priest we had at the time. He was my mentor. He lived what he preached. He walked the talk. His name was Thomas Connolly and he eventually became Bishop of Baker, Oregon. He was a builder and an avid horesman. He was passionate, compassionate, prayerful, forgiving, likable, hardworking and always willing to serve.

I would visit our local Church at night admiring the flickering red votive candles alight and the consoling figures of Jesus, Mary and Joseph, statues which gave me peace, permanency, consolation, and serenity. So, I decided to enter the high school seminary in Mt. View, California at 14; very young I know.

TWELVE YEARS OF BOARDING SCHOOL

I traveled by train alone and began a 12-year experience of high school, college, and theology. A late developer as far as girls were concerned, I did not dance or date. I had academics, athletics with few creative hobbies. I realized I was a square peg in a round hole since my entire education was memorizing facts and my small left brain found memorization difficult. Only later did I realize, I had an imaginative creative right brain seldom rewarded.

I endured this experience in high school, but in my senior year I couldn't keep up with Latin. I failed; they expelled me, so I went to a Catholic High School in Reno, Nevada and lived with my married older sister's family. I possessed excellent study habits, did very well, and graduated. I persisted in returning to seminary college at Mt. Angel Seminary outside Salem, Oregon, and my Bishop agreed to send me there.

Mt. Angel Seminary and Benedictine Abbey were separate but together and I did well there. It was claustrophobic in California and regimented. They had 310 rules, covering everything. I'm glad for the suffering and difficulty I experienced, and gained great discipline, motivation, and study habits.

"Ora et Labora" a Latin term meaning "Prayer and Work" which is a Benedictine motto as well as "treat all guests like Christ." I thrived in this environment. The seminary was separate from the monastery but the teachers were all monks. I studied 4 years of college in Philosophy and Psychology, and 4 more years of Theology including the Bible and elocution.

Again, it was all memorization and I had real difficulties remembering all this information. I was in a school where all the students were mostly left-brained, seldom art, some music, and not much in the field of imagination and creativity. I didn't realize that at the time, or would never have persisted.

Autobiography in Five Short Chapters

I

I walk down the street.
　　There is a deep hole in the sidewalk.
　　I fall in
　　I am lost . . . I am helpless
　　　　　It isn't my fault.
　　It takes forever to find a way out.

II

I walk down the same street.
　　There is a deep hole in the sidewalk.
　　I pretend I don't see it.
　　I fall in again.
I can't believe I am in the same place.
　　　　　　But it isn't my fault.
It still takes a long time to get out.

III

I walk down the same street.
There is a deep hole in the sidewalk.
　　I see it is there.
　　I still fall in . . . it's a habit.
　　　　　my eyes are open.
　　　　　I know where I am.

IV

I walk down the same street.
　　There is a deep hole in the sidewalk.
　　I walk around it.

V

I walk down another street.

　　　　　　　　　by: Portia Nelson

My old ancient tribe where I experience belonging and community.

Chapter Two

Right Brain Person Living In a Left Brain World

*We hold these truths to be self-evident;
All people are born creative; Endowed by our
Creator with the inalienable right
and responsibility to express our creativity
for the sake of ourselves and our world.*

—Barbara Marx Hubbard

I pulled to the side of the road, barely able to concentrate. This wasn't the first time that listening to songs on the radio caused vivid images to play through my consciousness like scenes in a movie. Nowadays, music videos are rampant. This was in the early 1970s, pre-MTV, when music was heard and not seen in non-musical images unless it accompanied a movie or a play.

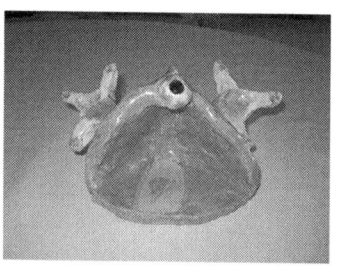

This one-eyed creature is actually a practical spoon holder

Clearly, I was right-brained; someone who thinks creatively, intuitively, holistically, and visually, rather than analytically and methodically as those who are left-brained do. Like Carl Jung, I was fascinated by symbols, colors, and shapes. I was drawn to use visuals in churches I served at a time when this was not done. I began to create popular TV spots for the Las Vegas, Nevada CBS affiliate.

First, though, I spent many years as a square peg trying to fit into a round hole in a left-brained world. The curriculum of the high school seminary that I attended sixteen years earlier in California revolved around memorizing facts. It didn't matter how hard I studied; I couldn't soak up facts. The faculty failed to inspire pathways of curiosity or wonder in me. School was regimented with hundreds of rules about everything from walking boundaries to behavioral limitations. How claustrophobic! Unfortunately, I failed to retain Latin translations, a dead language. I flunked and they expelled me. I finished my secondary education easily at a Catholic high school in Nevada, where I lived with my married sister.

Once again, God wrote straight with crooked lines. I am thankful because it was humbling and rearranged my place and space.

After graduation, I attended a college philosophy & theology program in a seminary near Salem, Oregon. I thrived in that environment. It was one of "Ora et labora"—-a Latin Benedictine motto for "pray and work". It taught you to treat everyone with hospitality as if they were Christ. All my teachers were monks. It was mostly memorization of facts but this time beautiful nature, animals, flowers, and sunsets enveloped us.

After studying liberal arts and philosophy for four years in college, I continued with four more years of theology. Again, it wasn't about creativity—no art, little music—but memorization. How could I ever remember all those dry facts? How could I compete with these left-brained students?

Some creative kids and adolescents never get over trying to contort their brains to work in ways that are unnatural for them. They dismiss their own strengths; doubt their intuition, constantly feeling like they never measure up. They may fall into despair and depression unless they discover their bliss and their passion.

As K.L. Toth says, "One of the greatest tragedies in life is to lose your own sense of self and accept the version of you that is expected by everyone else."

Somehow, my creativity and with it my sense of self flourished. My parents always encouraged me to discover my bliss, as long as I secured a good education. It was something that they ardently desired but did not have.

I was fortunate during my summers to work as a flagman for the Nevada Highway Department. A short time later, I worked for the Nevada Employment Department employing hay hands for ranches. I monitored enrollment in the Neighborhood Youth Corps, the Peace Corps, and other community action programs. In my spare time, I created collages based on various scriptures and placed them in the rear of my local Church for anyone to see. Looking back, it's clear that this was an expression of my right brain creativity.

Life itself pushed me in more creative directions. In 1968, I was ordained as a Catholic priest in my hometown. My parents were proud and elated.

Even so, I was still gullible, naive, and guileless. From a sheltered monastery on a hilltop distant from everyday people, my Bishop assigned me near the Las Vegas Strip.

The Strip was a phantasmagoria of pulsating attractions, entertainment, education, information, and excitement. It consisted of flickering neon signs, blaring sounds, stars singing, comedians joking, people dancing, and slot machines whirring. What a shock it was to my sense of normalcy.

While in the church looking at all the empty pews from the pulpit, I thought, "This is crazy! We're using a 13th century means of communication on a 20th century group of people."

My imagination soared and roared. My right brain allowed me to pivot and to step out of traditional methods of delivering sermons. I seized inspiration from my mentor, Marshall McLuhan, who famously said, "The medium is the message."

Marshall McLuhan was an insightful individual who did much more than teach communications at the University of Toronto from 1946 to 1979. He influenced generations of thoughtful individuals, including me. He showed us that the way something is communicated is just as powerful as the content. It could even be more important than the content that it was delivering like social media is today.

In the pulpit, we speak words and more words which generally lull people to sleep or trigger their own fantasies and daydreams. That is why Jesus spoke in parables, telling stories his followers could relate to.

I spontaneously began using visuals of all kinds—slides, films, overheads—at my services to teach the congregation. I used dialogue homilies with participant interactions. Congregants didn't need to memorize scriptures. I told real life stories to help them grow spiritually and I used tools and techniques to force them to relate themes to their everyday life.

In these early efforts, I turned to the Paulist, a religious order dedicated to modern communication. They pursued their mission by creating radio and TV spots and films by living in community. I began distributing their radio and TV spots to Las Vegas media stations. I got familiar with media managers and their staff. Then, the Las Vegas stations requested me to create, produce and distribute twenty, thirty, and sixty second spiritual spots with what at that time was called required free public service time.

With a reflex camera, I took slides of magazine images from Collier's, Life, Look, and Saturday Evening Post and turned them into slides.

I took two or three picture slides and added a short saying like, "God doesn't love you because you are good. You are good because God loves you!" In the lower corner, I would say, "This spot is brought to you by Loving Christians." These spots were played repeatedly on major stations as free public service announcements. There was no cost to anyone for this invaluable air time.

Another Twist and Turn in My Life

"You've got to go into the 8th grade class every Friday and teach them something," said my supervising pastor of the Catholic Church and School complex in Las Vegas where we both worked.

I said, "I don't think I'd like to do that."

And he said, "Well, you're going to."

Okay, I thought to myself. But I am not going to teach the way I was taught.

In the classroom, I had the students move their desks into five different groups of six.

"Here," I said, plopping magazines on their desks. "Pick a song that promotes the positives in humankind—peace, joy, justice, forgiveness, gratitude, loving kindness, and compassion."

Once each group picked their song, I asked them to tear out pictures to illustrate it.

"Your group has to agree on the song and the pictures. Whatever you create is fantastic."

Then I told them, "Now, I'm going to take these pictures and put them into slide form and we'll have a viewing of what you have accomplished."

"I was eventually able to get these slides shown on a local television show. Everyone was amazed that they were the creations of eighth graders."

PBS-TV Episodes

Then in 1970, I got a call from PBS in Las Vegas. With their sponsorship, I created a six-episode family-oriented show called "Family Matters". In those episodes, I would play a twenty-minute movie produced by the Franciscan Communication Center in Los Angeles. Each movie dealt with a challenging family situation.

Following the movie presentation, I interviewed local people who were dealing with challenges similar to those exhibited in the movie. These challenges included drug addiction, alcoholism, grief and dying, communication difficulties, and topics involving peace and social justice, or ethics and morality. This program series became so successful that other TV stations rebroadcasted them.

At the same time, I was given access to thirty minutes of public service time on Top 40 Radio program and fifteen minutes of public service time on a local Modern Country music station. Both time slots were available on Sundays.

Again, I wasn't going to preach on radio in the traditional way. I commented on the songs that I had selected and related it to a common theme. For every minute I talked, I played three minutes of music on a particular topic. My audience was not tribal, not identified with any particular religion, so I kept the message universal, through music. The medium was radio. The messages were current songs synchronized to a theme. It was entertaining and informal.

The Power of Media

To illustrate the power of this medium, I wish to draw your attention to two true stories:

Fast forward ten or twelve years. I was in the Northern Nevada desert visiting an old mining town. The ranger at the state park said, "I recognize your voice."

"Were you ever in Las Vegas?" I asked.

"Yeah, that's where it was," he said. "My mother forbade us from listening to Rock 'N Roll on Sundays, but she said we could listen to you."

This was the perfect medium for me because I am an introvert. I talked alone in a sound proof booth.

On a second occasion, I was speaking to a radio station general manager. I said, "You know I'm on Sunday mornings at 8:00am. How many people do you think are listening?"

"Not many," he said.

"How many is not many?" I queried.

"Maybe 50,000." he responded.

Fifty thousand! This radio program reached more people than attended all the churches, synagogues, and mosques in the entire State of Nevada. People I didn't know were listening and involved in a new way of understanding and communicating. I was in the right place, time and doing the correct thing with what I now know is my active right brain. I found a modern way to communicate easily to the masses and it cost nothing.

In so doing, I followed the advice of my secular college speech teacher:

"Tell them what you're going to say. Say it! Then tell them you said it. You have to grab their attention with the first sentence out of your mouth. You've got seven minutes because you're competing with the likes of Walter Cronkite and the rest of those reporters and actors. Remember, in their minds they're cooking dinner, playing a game or replaying a sports event. You have to grab, and hold their attention and interest for seven minutes. Can you do that?"

If we went over seven minutes, our teacher flunked us with a thumbs down. "I don't care how good your speech was!" "It was too long!", he would explain. Believe me, it was a very challenging and humbling experience.

I took this to heart in my TV spots and sermons. Even my content was different. I didn't believe in literalism. I did not believe some of the events of the Bible literally happened. Rather than memorizing rules and platitudes, I guided my congregation to dive deeper into scriptures and what it meant to them personally.

Hebrew rabbis and scholars sometimes use a method called Midrash to reflect on a story and to communicate all of its underlying message. Midrash is the process of consistently using questions to keep spiritual meanings open.

Understanding Scripture

How can you understand scripture? It can be understood on at least four levels of meaning: Literal, deep, comparative, and hidden, as another mentor, Richard Rohr, OFM, says in his book entitled Jesus and the Bible.

"The **literal** level of meaning doesn't get to the root and, in fact, is the least helpful to the soul and the most dangerous from history," he writes.

"**Deep** meaning offers symbolic or allegorical applications.

Comparative study combines different texts to explore an entirely new meaning.

Finally, in traditional Jewish exegesis, **hidden** meaning gets at the Mystery itself.

Midrash allows and encourages each listener to grow with a text and not settle for mere literalism, which, of itself, bears little spiritual fruit. It is just a starting point."

Reading Biblical stories and parables is like peeling a banana to get to the fruit of the matter. You can use this 'peeling' process to read this book, write your own story or live your own life with gusto.

For instance, in the Gospel of Matthew Chapter 25: 14-30, Jesus told the following parable about a manager who leaves on a trip. Before leaving, he puts three of his servants in charge of his property and gives to each one a sum of money to manage according to their ability. To the first servant, he gives five thousand dollars. To the second servant, he gives two thousand dollars. And, to the third servant, he gives one thousand dollars. Then, the property manager went on his trip. He instructed the servants to take the money that they had been given and go forth and creatively multiply it during his absence.

When the manager returned, he found that the first two servants had invested their money and doubled it. Each of these two servants was rewarded with more responsibility. The third servant during the manager's absence had gone off, dug a hole in the ground and hid the manager's money because he was afraid of losing it. Learning of this lack of increase in the original amount, the manager became angry with the third servant, condemned him, and relieved him of his station.

After relating this parable, I asked my listeners, "Why did the manager give the money to the servants? It didn't seem to matter what they did as long as they did something? Did it matter at all what they did? I was greeted with a deafening silence.

I said to the congregation, "Look under the pew. Some of you will discover money down there."

They looked excitedly. Someone found a ten-dollar bill, another got a five-dollar bill, and someone got a one-dollar bill.

I said, "You've heard the parable. Now I challenge you to do what you want with the money, and then report back to us next week about what happened."

They did some really creative things. One gave his money to a soup kitchen and volunteered there, too. Others shared it with the Red Cross or Habitat for Humanity.

That's how I got their attention. I believe that adults grow spiritually through real life situations and experiences. I challenged them to grasp these readings, stories and parables in a new way. How does it affect our lives right now? Then, they have to respond always with positive creative actions.

I realized we need to stop being linear, and start being wholistic. What I was doing—-and I didn't know this at the time—-was expanding their soul consciousness. They were surprised. Most of these people came from the Eastern or Northeastern United States. They were used to boring sermons that put them to sleep. They drifted off or escaped some place in their brains to daydream. They were busy paying off installments on their so-called religious fire insurance policy. By engaging in endlessly repetitive mental prayers and devotions, they believed that they were sure to pile up enough grace along with good deeds to get into Heaven. Such behavior resulted from an assumed religious bargain between themselves and a fearful, accountant-like God.

I never judged this misguided preoccupation but I could see that I was there to give them both content and new methods of understanding. I strived to alter their imbedded perceptions so they would get excited about the evolved meaning of their religious beliefs. I was just the messenger. How they responded was up to them.

A New Chapter in a New Location

After eight years in Las Vegas, my Bishop assigned me as pastor to a parish in Carson City, Nevada, the State Capitol of Nevada. At 110 years old, the church was built during the Virginia City Silver Rush in the 1860s. The inside walls of the church were so old that they leaned outward. Fortunately, they were held in place by strong steel cables preventing their collapse.

Every Sunday the church was so packed, people had to stand outside beyond the vestibule. Originally built for a total population of 2,000, the City had grown to roughly 30,000 people. Few before me had looked into expansion or rebuilding as there were so little funds to do so.

In Las Vegas, I learned about the necessary tithing of the first tenth of 100% of a parishioner's time, talent, and treasure. I knew I couldn't begin any work on the church unless we increase our income. During the previous year prior to my assignment, the total annual donations amounted to only $75,000.

This is crazy with a population like this! I thought. The majority of these people are middle class working for the State government. I explained to them it's not just about money. You can give your time or your talent and not give any treasure. As long as you could pull the dandelions in the lawn or cut a cord of wood or do some maintenance and gardening, your tithing obligation is considered fulfilled. A third of the parishioners were inspired enough to sign up to donate their tithe. Then, I used to say, "If you can't do that, you can give an hour of your salary a week." That eliminated the dollar in the collection plate mentality.

I revolutionized their consciousness. I expanded their experience about scriptures, goals and hopes. I increased the whole physical, mental, emotional, and spiritual aspects of the community.

If they thought small, I taught them to think BIG!

We looked around for land on which to build a new church but we couldn't find anything suitable. It was either the wrong place or the wrong price.

Then, by happy synchronicity, I talked to a man, who happened to be a contractor, who said, "We can expand the church in the back, increase the capacity in the balcony, and add a basement for a social hall. We'll double the space for a lot less!"

"Okay, draw up the plans," I said. I didn't know a contractor from an architect at the time. But I had additional assistance from others. We accomplished the expansion task in six months, all of it paid for with tithing pledges. The congregation expanded not only their building but their inner awareness. Change your attitude, change your thinking! Change your thinking, change your behavior!

Every October I used an overhead projector to give them a financial report of what we'd done the previous year. I called it, "A Sermon on the Amount!"

During that first year of tithing, contributions doubled to $150,000.

"We're going to use these pledges for this expansion," I told them. "I believe, like the Mormons do, that when we build this building and turn the key, it will be paid for. We're not going to have a church debt or a mortgage to burn years from now. We're going to pledge to cover the entire cost of the project."

I gave them a money back guarantee. If they didn't receive blessings from whatever they gave, I would personally return what they had given. I meant it. I don't remember anyone asking for a rebate. I also told them they could examine our yearly financial records. Giving and receiving is really the same thing.

Giving and Receiving

Then, we also tithed 10% of our income to the poor in Nevada, the Nation and the World. We showed our parishioners that their potential collectively was much more than 10% on multiple levels. When you give in trust, you reap much more personally and collectively.

I stayed with that church from 1976 to 1981. After the completion of this assignment, I needed a rest. I recommended an excellent clerical associate to the Bishop who subsequently took the reins.

Twenty years after I left this church, the parishioners sold the Church, the clergy living quarters and the social hall. With those funds, they were donated 40 acres of land and built a much larger Church, a new clergy residence, office space, a social hall and a small chapel for weekday services, funerals and weddings. This demonstrates what tithing and a new perspective will do!

Do Some Personal Exploration

Explore what changes are needed in your life. What in your life needs expansion, revision, or change? What are your hopes, desires, reflections, and dreams? Examine your present for a better future.

On the left-hand side of a sheet of paper list your regrets, sadness, depressions, despair, and losses. On the right side of the paper list your successes, hopes, desires, dreams, opportunities, talents, and gifts. Expand your possibilities. Look at the tools, techniques and tricks below.
Note: For more on the Left Brain/Right Brain check out: The Brain from Top to Bottom by Bruno Dubuc, a neuroscientist at McGill University.

Take the Left Brain/Right Brain Test

Just a reminder: categories like right brain/left brain are not meant to be boxes. They are portals into well-being and illumination. If an aha! light bulb goes off when introduced to a new way of thinking, play with it and see what you discover. If there are no new insights, let it go.

Pick a pivotal moment or two from your life. It can be a story you've told others again and again or it can be a story you've only told yourself.

Treat it as a parable, dream, vision or scripture. Use **Midrash** to explore it. What is its **literal** meaning? What is its **contemplative** meaning? What is its hidden meaning?

Again, there are no mistakes. Trust whatever arises in you as you explore.

Turn it into a collage, drawing, painting, doodle, or simply collect and cut out images from magazines that express what words cannot. What song or melody cuts to the heart of your experience? Express it in ceramics or macrame like I did in this book or whatever hobby, you enjoy.

As for Tithing—-For whom or what do you tithe in your life? Which people or places inspire you? What has it brought into your life? I invite you to tithe—-to persons you want to support, or to an organization. Tithing is for everyone for everything. Sometimes it's buying a meal for someone else by paying it forward. Do whatever inspires you. It is rewarding in many ways!

*This ceramic began as a pig
and transformed into a hippopotamus*

DO YOU WANT TO BE FREE?

Being here could be a growth opportunity, an opportunity to become the best you can be in life!

"If you always do what you always done, you will always get what you always got."

"If nothing changes, nothing changes!"

Here are some simple tools for inner freedom. Use what works for you:

- AFFIRMATIONS – On the left side of the paper write out all the negative things said to you growing up. On the right side of the paper translate the negatives to POSITIVE phrases and say these affirmations daily (even if you don't believe them).
- GRIEF – Make a list of the losses in your life – people, places, and situations. Number them in order – greatest loss to lesser losses. Take #1 and write a grief letter. Feel the pain and release it!
- ANGER – The things we are most unaware of in ourselves is what makes us so very ANGRY when we see them in other people or situations. Someone here will push our buttons and we will get ANGRY. STOP and ask yourself who does that person or situation remind me of in my past childhood and experience? Begin to deal with the pain

and feelings there.
- DREAMS – Write them down after waking up and learn the tools to decode the message for you. "Everything in the dream is about you, and you are the best interpreter of your own dreams."
- LIST FOR YOURSELF:
  - 50 GOALS
  - 150 BLESSINGS
  - 50 Persons you LISTEN to
- ELIMINATE ALL BLAME
- ELIMINATE ALL CRITICISM
- ELIMINATE ALL JUDGEMENTS
- ELIMINATE ALL GOSSIP AND RUMORS
- ELIMINATE ALL SHAME AND GUILT
- ELIMINATE ALL COMPLAINTS

These will make you very sick!
Take care of your life. Take RESPONSIBILITY for your own BEHAVIOR NOW!

- LEARN THE SYMPTOMS OF CODEPENDENCY and POSITIVE ways to ASSERT YOURSELF.
- GET A POWER GREATER THAN YOURSELF and learn the tools to CONTACT that HIGHER POWER.

Chapter Three

All Therapy is Grief Therapy

*Deep grief sometimes is almost like a specific
location, a coordinate on a map of time.
When you are standing in that forest of sorrow,
you cannot imagine that you could ever find your
way to a better place. But if someone can assure you
that they themselves have stood in that same place,
and now have moved on, sometimes this
will bring hope.*

—Elizabeth Gilbert, "Eat, Pray, Love"

Cancer" and "spreading" are words no one wants to hear in the same sentence. Amy and I were newlyweds, married for just a month, when she was diagnosed with breast cancer. She was 50 years old. I was 59. For me, crossing the threshold from being a priest for 31 years to being a husband was happily disorienting. Too quickly, though, I became a caregiver, tending to the woman I loved as she faced chemotherapy and then a year of radiation treatments.

After my new wife finished all her treatments, her doctor told her she would likely be able to enjoy ten cancer-free years. Ten years is better than ten months, weeks, days. But how does the human heart make sense of such a pronouncement?

Amy and I made a pact to live our lives as positively, in-the-moment as possible. We wanted to engage in deep, meaningful moments together because of our limited time together. (Of course, we are all here for a limited time.) How do you live in the world of daily to-dos and the extraordinary and sometimes terrifying Mystery simultaneously?

We traveled to Spain and Italy, breathing in the air of Tuscany where my father was born. We took in all the beauty of Canada by train. Then we returned to Amy's family roots in St. Paul, Minnesota.

Together she and I tasted a multitude of living conditions, savoring new people, flavors, philosophies and geographies. None of that would have been possible if we hadn't taken the time to consciously navigate our revolving emotions and sensations—shock, powerlessness, joy, anger, gratitude, sadness, exhaustion, anxiety, and peace.

Many of you may know Dr. Elisabeth Kubler-Ross, a pioneer of the hospice movement, and the identifier of the five stages of grief/dying: shock, denial, bargaining, anger, and acceptance (not necessarily in that order). Anyone who has plunged into the altered state of grief knows that it is natural to pivot between multiple emotions in one day, one afternoon, or even one hour. Grief is not linear. And we don't just grieve death. Most people, I have found, carry tremendous amounts of grief without even realizing it. (No one can tell you something is not worth grieving over. It's your grief!)

Chances are you have been faced with a few of these common grief issues/losses:

- Death of a primary caregiver (i.e. a parent, relative, or parental figure) as a child or as an adult.
- Loss of relationship with a parent or primary caregiver through physical or emotional absence or neglect.
- Loss of a recent or significant relationship in the past such as with a spouse, lover, close friend, or a child leaving home.

- Loss of a child, either through death, or loss of relationship. (i.e.. adoptions, miscarriages, abortions, stillbirths).
- Loss of a significant employment, military service, or hobby.
- Death or lost relationship with a sibling, relative, or friend with whom you were particularly close.
- Loss of special pets as a child or as an adult.
- Loss of health, bodily function, or a limb.
- Loss of dreams, beliefs, or paradigms.
- Loss of job, home, or school.

During her psychiatric residency in the late 1950s, Dr. Kubler-Ross was mortified by the way doctors treated dying patients. Her book Death and Dying, launched a necessary cultural conversation around this previously taboo topic. Thanks to her and others like her, our society is becoming increasingly more candid about death, failures and other losses. Yet unspoken and often unconscious desires about how we and others should grieve linger: Get over it, we tell others or ourselves—whatever IT may be—in a reasonable way in a reasonable amount of time.

One woman couldn't believe her best friend was

still grieving her mother's death after seven weeks. Then a few months later, her own mother died suddenly, and she understood.

Our friends and family don't always know how to sit with us in our grief. Their responses don't mean we don't deserve support. They mean we need to seek comfort somewhere else. That's why it's important to reach out for support where you can. That is especially true for boys and men, who are trained by schools, sports, families, and friendships to suppress or deny any vulnerability.

Fortunately, Amy and I knew better than to attempt to handle our challenges alone. We sought wisdom from counselors, social workers, and friends on their own cancer journeys. The Marriage Encounters we both attended and I facilitated helped us get into our feelings, as mentioned in Chapter 7: Relationship is Life.

Amy wondered why I couldn't intuit her thoughts and feelings. I subsequently learned how to pay attention to nonverbal communication—visual cues, voice intonation, and facial expressions while listening to her personal dreams and feelings. A social worker assisted me.

Thankfully, grace put me in the right place at the correct time. My work as a hospice chaplain during her illness and my Clinical Pastoral Education Trainings (CPE) gave me the skills needed as I required them. In addition to cultivating compassion, intuition and patience, I learned how to truly listen to other people. All of this helped me become an improved caregiver for Amy. Most persons don't have the luxury of this preparation.

Unexpected Transitions

"What are you going to do next?" Amy asked after I'd completed my year-long CPE training at a Hospital.

"I'm just sitting around praying and waiting to see what the next step is," I replied.

Soon, a chaplain who worked at a hospice began asking me to fill in for him. Eventually, I found a full-time position at a hospice. I ultimately worked there for seven years. While there, I rediscovered that hospice caregivers and family members caring for their loved ones required a more comprehensive vision of what hospice provides.

Say 'hospice care' and most people think of doctors, nurses, and caregivers. There is so much more involved, which inspired me to create this hospice pie circle shown here. My intent has always been to give caregivers and patients tools to help them reach some kind of serenity, safety, security and tranquility in the midst of such intensity.

Hospice Total Map

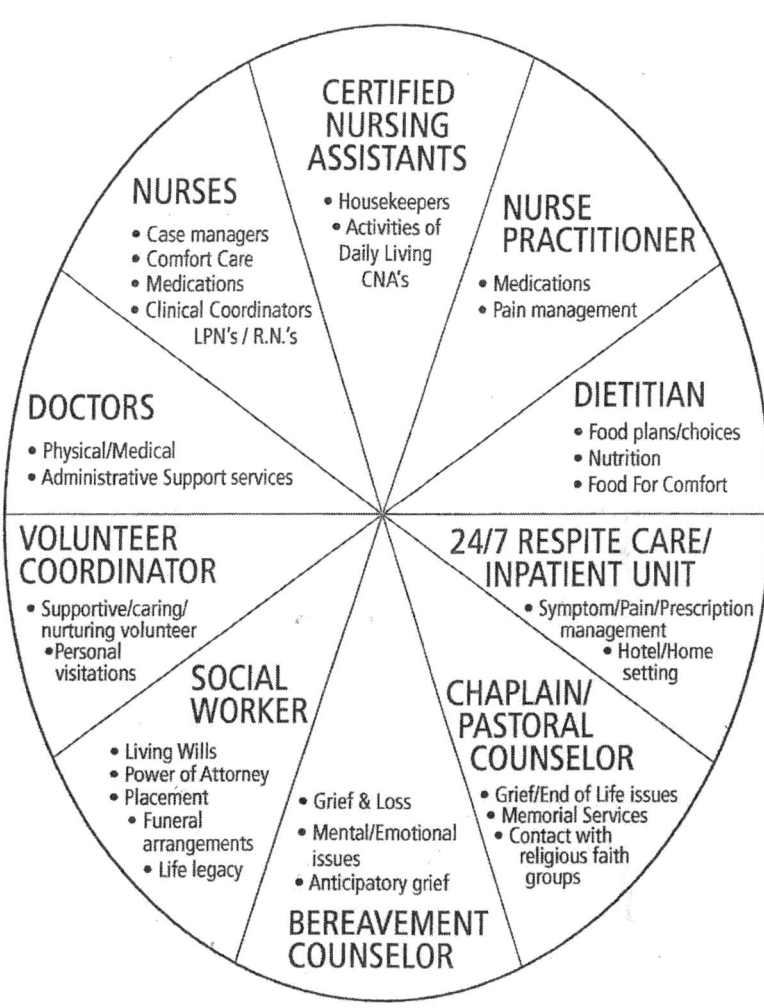

I also developed a caregiver packet, which included self-reflection questions for caregivers. Caregiving is all-encompassing. Because the focus is on the loved one's needs, the caregiver runs the risk of losing connection with their own spiritual and bodily needs. Self-care and self-nurturing can feel narcissistic instead of life-saving. That's why all hospices offer caregivers respite.

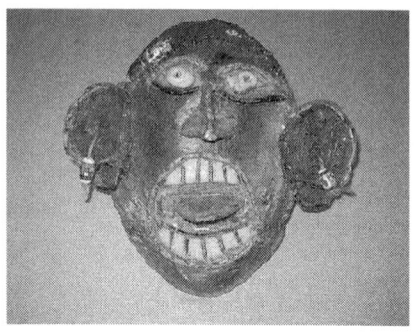

*Ceramic of Maori Warrior mask
who are in touch with grief and grieving*

During such a respite, the patient receives care at an inpatient unit for five days every six weeks. The caregiver can then travel, stay home, visit family and friends, or do whatever they desire, to restore clarity, and invite deep physical, mental, spiritual and emotional rest back into their own lives.

Caregiving Challenges

"If you are a caregiver, you can ascertain your current caregiving status by answering the following questions taken from the American Academy of Bereavement Training Manual."

Are you burning out?

What changes have you noticed in yourself and the world around you, in your work place, family, or social situations?

Answer the following questions and assign each a number within a range from 1 to 5 to designate the degree of change that you perceive (1 for little or no change up to a maximum of 5 for a great deal of change).

- Do you tire more easily? Are you feeling more fatigued than energetic?
- Are people telling you, "You don't look so good lately?"
- Are you working harder and accomplishing less?
- Do you feel increasingly disenchanted by life?
- Do you notice yourself being cynical about life?

- Are you more forgetful than usual about appointments? Are you increasingly irritable? Short-tempered? More disappointed in people around you?
- Are you engaging with close friends and family members less than usual?
- Are you too busy to do ordinary things like make phone calls, read reports or drop a line to friends and family?
- Are you suffering from physical complaints (aches, pains, headaches, colds?)
- Do you feel a letdown at the end of the day?
- Is joy a forgotten feeling?
- Are you unable to laugh at a joke about yourself?
- Do you feel trapped in your job situation?
- Do you have very little to say to people?
- Is your day filled with too much repetition?
- Do you sense that your work is meaningless?
- Is sex more trouble than it's worth?
- Do you feel interpersonal conflict with co-workers or family?
- Do you have no opportunity for self-motivated time outs?

While we can all benefit by being gentler with ourselves, the higher your total score, the greater the need for corrective action. Burnout is reversible, no matter how severe in the moment. Consider taking this quiz your first step to addressing your burnout. Hospice staff and hospital social workers are great resources for finding the care you need. You can find relief!

Add up your individual scores from above and compare the total sum to the categories below:

- *0-25*: You are doing well.
- *26-35*: Be mindful. Keep checking inside about your well-being.
- *36-50*: You are becoming a candidate for burnout.
- *51-65*: You are burning out!
- *65+*: You are in a dangerous place, that is threatening to your physical, emotional, mental and spiritual well-being.

ATTITUDE ADJUSTMENTS

When in doubt, ask questions. Inquiry is a powerful tool to break through ancient, unhealthy ways of thinking, feeling, or acting. It can initiate positive transformation.

In hospice, when a dying patient would ask,

"Why is God doing this to me?" I'd say, "Tell me about your God."

They would inevitably describe a negative, punishing, vengeful God.

I'd say, "Okay, how is this concept of God working out for you?"

"Well, not very well at all!" the patient would reply.

"Have you ever considered firing that God and getting a new one?" I would ask.

That was sometimes a shocking thought. The patient would often respond, "I've never thought about that!"

I would suggest, "Well, reflect on that."

How moving it is to witness people imagine a new God, one radiating unconditional love. This change of perspective liberates them from the fear of eternal punishment in the hereafter. It fed my spirit to expand their soul consciousness with fresh awareness's, choices, and decisions.

Life is What Happens When You Are Making Other Plans

True to doctor's prediction, ten years after Amy stopped chemotherapy, her cancer reappeared and began to metastasize. It changed its form and went after her bone. The doctor reevaluated her status and determined that she had only 18 months to live.

One morning Amy could hear me in the family room, crying.

"What is going on?" she asked.

"I was missing you," I said. "Remembering the things that we shared, feeling sad with grief, trying to let go."

She understood and we held each other. Later, we listened to John Denver songs which expressed our hopes, dreams, and feelings. They allowed our grief, relief, and a sense of peace to flow.

Everyone grieves differently and that's okay. Some people talk to someone they trust. Others process quietly. Some stay busy; others are called to silence. We all need generous doses of self-compassion during such a fragile time. Everything anyone does or says penetrates that much more deeply than normal.

The important thing is to give yourself the dignity of acknowledging and expressing your emotions as best you can. Don't blame yourself for feeling sad, sorry, numb or angry. Don't try to force yourself to rush your process. Feelings are not distractions. They are messengers worthy of your attention. If unexpressed, they won't disappear. They'll hide, fester, and possibly manifest as physical illnesses or addictions.

Having the courage to face your feelings allows you to move through the grief of any loss. Trust me, one day you will find yourself laughing. The sense of yearning for whoever or whatever was lost, will diminish. It will return, then diminish and possibly flare up again. It will transpire in your own unique rhythm, for as long as it takes, while you grow stronger. All the while, you will develop into, not your old self, but a new more vibrant, resilient self.

Note: To assist in your grief journey, every Hospice and some Churches, Hospitals, and mortuaries offer free grief groups to attend. Just ask! I found them terrifically helpful. Write the generic grief letter below as a starter. I discovered that most movies, TV, theater, and novels deal with unresolved grief while experiencing unnecessary intense suffering, pain and dead-end destructive behaviors.

After Amy died, I was, naturally, sad, but not destroyed. It helped me immensely to have written her an anticipatory grief letter. As time went on, I allowed myself to play music we both enjoyed. I was able to pour over pictures of our travels and celebrations together. Eventually I was able to write about our common memories. Ultimately, I carved out a different life, but with her now as an integral part of me. This book is a practical expression.

It takes strength to make your way through grief, to grab hold of life and let it pull you forward.

—Patti Davis

A Sample Grief Letter

This is a terrific generic grief letter that I recommend to others. I use it for my own losses.

A grief letter allows you to express everything you need to show to the person or situation of your choice, whether they be living or departed. People often experience a deeper sense of wholeness, relief, and release after writing such a grief letter. There's no guarantee you'll experience any of those things, but you will probably feel an inner shift or movement of your perspective.

There is no wrong or right way to write your grief letter. It is deeply personal. Who do you want to write it to? Your Mother? Father? Husband? Wife? Child? Friend? Colleague? Grandparent? Start where you are. You may have intense emotion as you write, or no feelings at all. Wherever you are, is right where you need to be. This is not a time to be politically correct, polite, or tactful. Just pay attention to what is rising within you and keep writing. Your letter is as short or long as you need. Write it in one setting or take breaks and return to it. Then if you wish, share it with a trusted friend or professional.

Here are some guidelines to get you started; take what you want and add or subtract the rest:

Dear _____

I resent you for _____

I appreciate you for _____

I'm sorry that _____

I feel sad that _____

I did not get enough _____

I thank you for _____

I am angry at you for _____

What I miss most about you is _____

All I ever wanted from you was _____

I regret I never told you _____

I forgive you for _____

I love you for _____

I am happy that _____

I am grateful _____

CREATE A TIMELINE

If you are not ready to dive into your letter, create a timeline of your relationship to the person, job, pet, or experience. Focus on the loss that is most present to you, that has the most charge. Commit the memories, be they happy, sad, silly, or challenging, to paper or onto a computer. Yes, this is a timeline, but embrace whatever memories come. They don't have to be in order. If no memories emerge from a particular loss, shift your focus to another loss, and see what happens.

Special Circumstances: Stillbirth, Adoption, Abortion

Imagine or recall the age, sex, and name of your child. In your letter, share with your child your life circumstances around the time of your loss and your decision to abort, or give them up for adoption. Tell your child what you might have hoped for in a relationship with them. Say everything. This is important for fathers as well as for mothers.

The Gift of Saying Goodbye

Letting go of a loved one or pet that has died or acknowledging that the job or marriage is no more allows your deep energy of grief to shift. It also allows your inherent sense of aliveness to emerge. There is power in saying goodbye to the guilt, the shame, the anguish, the remorse, the horror, the anger and the incapacitation of any relationship or situation. And in the end, you get to keep all the love and happy memories.

What if you don't want to let go? What if you don't want to say goodbye? Express as much as you can, layer by layer. I can't emphasize enough that unexpressed grief will express itself somewhere in your life, often in trauma or illness. Expressing allows you to gather new meaning, relatedness, forgiveness, purpose and hope for the future.

We grow strong in the broken places of our lives when and if we grieve. Our Creator writes straight with crooked lines.

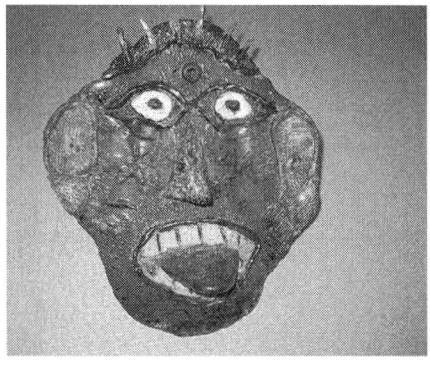

Scary Maori Mask Showing Anger, Fear, and Grief

Suggested Resources to Google and Expand

Five Wishes (fivewishes.org) is a complete approach to discussing and documenting your care and comfort choices. It's about connecting families, communicating with healthcare providers, and showing your community what it means to care for one another.

"The Mask You Live In" a video documentary by Jennifer Siebel Newsome.
For all those with PTSD: Post Traumatic Stress Disorder. Experiencing Global Warming, Pandemic Viruses, Physical, Emotional, Religious, Sexual, or Mental Abuses. Veterans in the Military, War, Police, Politics, Black Lives Matter, Rape, Racism, Bigotry and other Survivors of Constant Stressful Vocations or Situations.

These two below may resolve the above experiences:
EFT: Emotional Freedom Technique web site. It involves "tapping" to release stress, grief, anxiety, or other debilitating feelings. Anyone can learn and do it to themselves.

EMDR: Eye Movement Desensitization Reprocessing. This involves a trained therapist to reconnect your left and right brain by unscrambling your stuck brain over past traumatic events. There are no pills, no medicines, no hypnosis, no chicanery. I have experienced both of them, and they worked for me.

Question: Do you wish to eliminate whinnying, moaning, groaning, sniveling, complaining, and criticizing from your life? Then work the exercises in this book diligently, and be amazed!

FIFTEEN RULES FOR FAIR, INTIMATE DISCUSSION

1. Be specific when you introduce a gripe.
2. Dont just complain, no matter how specifically; ask for a reasonable change that will relieve
3. Ask for and give feedback for the major points to make sure you are heard, to assure your partner that you understand what he/she wants.
4. Confine yourself to one issue at a time. Otherwise, without professional guidance, you may skip back and forth, evading the hard ones.
5. Do not be glib or intolerant. Be open to your own feelings, and equally open to your partner's.
6. Always consider compromise and negotiation. Remember, your partner's view of reality may be just as real as yours, even though yours may differ. There are not many totally objective realities.
7. Do not allow counter-demands to enter the picture until the original demands are clearly understood and responded to.
8. Never assume that you know what your partner is thinking until you have checked out the assumption in plain language. Never assume nor predict how he/she will react, what he/she will reject.
9. Don't assault. Ask. Do not correct a partner of his/her own feelings. Do not tell a partner what he/she should know, do, or feel.
10. Never put labels on a partner. Call him/her neither a coward, nor a neurotic, nor a child. If you

really believe that he/she was incompetent or suffered from some hopeless basic flaw, you probably would not be with him/her. Do not make sweeping, labeling judgements about feelings, especially about whether or not they are real or important.

11. Sarcasm is dirty fighting.
12. Forget the past and stay with the here-and-now. What either of you did last year, last month, or that morning is not as important as what you are doing and feeling now. And the changes you ask cannot possibly be retroactive. Hurts, grievances, and irritations should be brought up at the very earliest moment, or the partner has the right to suspect that they may have been said carefully as a weapon.
13. Do not overload your partner with grievances. To do so makes him/her feel hopeless and suggests that you have either been hoarding complaints or have not thought through what really troubles you.
14. Meditate. Take time to consult your real thoughts and feelings before speaking. Your surface reactions may mask something deeper and more important. Don't be afraid to close your eyes and just think.
15. Remember that there is never a single winner in an honest intimate discussion; both either win more intimacy or lose it.

Chapter Four

How to Massage a Dream

Another useful tool that I have discovered in my quest for a better understanding of myself and my life is dream analysis.

> *A dream not understood is like*
> *a letter not opened.*
> —The Talmud

I am at a Jungle Endurance Training Center in the middle of the desert, with my Jeep buried in the sand. I am free to leave at any time but I have important lessons to learn. Contrary to all appearances, I am not stuck.

That's the dream I had after I applied for a prison chaplain's job. It was a job that I actually did not want to undertake.

As a child and as a teenager, I did not take dreams seriously. Thanks to Carl Jung, the pioneer of analytical psychology, I have since embraced dreams as powerful messengers, and not scrambled, nonsensical images from our psyche. According to Jung, "The symbol in a dream has more the value of a parable; it does not conceal, it teaches."

When faced with pivotal choices, dreams have always shown me the way. While discussing my Jungle Endurance Training dream with a friend, he revealed that Jungle Environment was another term for prison. That piece of information was key to unlocking the dream's meaning for me. I accepted the prison chaplain job knowing that the job is valuable and not wasting my time or resources. I realized that I was not trapped, but could leave at any time.

I invite you to bring a dream to mind and hold it in your consciousness as you read on. You don't need to do anything with it right now. Just let it hang out. Know that playing in the field of your dreams yields rich rewards. Dreams have the potential to teach, affirm, direct and enlighten. They are especially potent because they are created from our own unique vocabulary of images. Sometimes dreams are the only way vital, beneficial information penetrates us.

"Again and again I find that my own inner counselor; my secret dreaming self, is not only wise and helpful but usually amusing as well," says Sheldon Kopp, author of The Hanged Man. Beginning to trust your dreams and your interpretation of them is a process. I've repeatedly experienced that my fork-in-the-road dreams are here to alert me. They show me what I will encounter in the future and how I'll need to deal with it.

After 18 months as a chaplain at the state prison, I applied for a federal prison job located in northern Phoenix, Arizona. The group that interviewed me said they wanted to hire me. Once again, I wasn't sure I wanted to take the job, even with a raise in salary.

My uncertainty inspired my Eagle Arrow Dream:

I am at a mountain cabin. Behind it is a lean-to, normally used for storing wood for the fireplace. When I dig into the wood pile, though, I pull out a burlap sack filled with gold coins. Imprinted on each gold coin is an eagle with its talons wrapped around a bundle of arrows.

I recorded my dream in my dream journal and put it aside. I've kept a dream journal for 50 years. Sometimes I write my dreams down if I awaken in the middle of my normal sleep cycle. Mostly, I record them early in the morning upon waking up because the memory of the dream is still fresh. Later in the day, in the margins I may write comments, conclusions, connections, symbols or revelations and discover deeper meanings for me. It's an invaluable tool.

After the Eagle Arrow dream, I attended two weeks of instructional sessions on procedures and policies at the prison.

I couldn't help but see the Bureau of Prisons' insignia on the training facility wall. What image did it boast? It was an eagle with its talons wrapped around a bundle of arrows—identical to the one that I saw imprinted on the gold coins in my dream. I interpreted that to mean, "Treat these inmates like gold coins. Treat them with respect and honor." That realization led to my knowing that I was in the correct place at the right time. I didn't know how long I'd be there, but that's where I was to use my talents for now.

It is my understanding that only 10% of our dreams are prophetic, like the Eagle Arrow Dream. The rest are journey dreams guiding us in dealing with life's choices, hopes, desires, hurdles, challenges and curve balls.

Even so-called nightmares are useful. Just as in

waking life, when we refuse to listen to messages Life gives us, the information increases. As dream-worker Jeremy Taylor says, "All dreams speak a universal language and come in the service of health and wholeness. There is no such thing as a bad dream. Dreams that take on a dramatic or repetitive form only occur in order to grab our attention."

After my retirement, I devoured the local Parks and Recreation magazine and signed up for talks, seminars, line dancing, square dancing, yoga, and things I'd never tried before. I challenged myself to experience all that they had to offer.

Then this Potluck dream came to me:

I arrive at a potluck in a church hall. As we all know, at a potluck you get to choose what you want to eat from a bounty of food. The kids had already chosen Mac and Cheese and sugary desserts. The adults had also chosen their food and sat around eating. "Where is my food", I wondered? I look around and could only find dribbles and drabbles of food. I sit down, thinking, "We'll see what happens." When I look up, I see a man dressed as a waiter in the doorway. In the palm of his hand he holds a tray with a plate of food on it. He walks through the doorway, heads right toward me and puts the plate down in front of me. Then he bows and leaves.

I played with the symbols. A potluck is all about give and take. Typically, you bring food to share and also eat what someone else has brought. Everyone wanders around a table of goodies to select whatever appeals to them. This time, I would not actively choose which foods I wished. I would wait, trusting my Higher Power to deliver all the food that I needed. This waiting was a test of my ability to trust the present as well as a foreshadowing my future. I was to wait for what was to be delivered to me and to let events unfold. This insight proved to be both accurate and beneficial.

Allow me to challenge you to experience all that your dreams have to offer. I encourage you to begin your dream work and dream play by taking the dream you have held in mind—or any other dream

The Dreamworld is Like Rainbow Fishing

that comes forth—and explore and analyze it. Experiment with various techniques until you find what works best for you.

"This process of analysis has been termed 'dream diving'. The sequence of the exercise goes as follows:"

DREAM DIVING

- Create a title for your dream.
- Theme: In one sentence sum up the theme or themes of the dream. There is no one right answer. This isn't like picking a theme for an essay or short story in school. This is your dream. The theme may emerge after you have explored it over time.
- Feelings: Explore any feelings that arose in the dream. Was the overall feeling tone fear? Love? Confidence? Confusion? Did it shift over the course of the dream?
- Senses: What did you see? Hear? Sense? Smell? Taste? Touch?
- Images: Spend time with images from the dream such as those of people, animals, buildings, and colors. Ask how the images relate to you, to your life, and to others in your life.

Note: Play with recording or sharing your dreams in the present tense. The immediacy can make the dream experience more potent and alive, and filled with details otherwise forgotten.

Dreams As Questions

Instead of providing direct answers, the role of some dreams may be to ask questions that catalyze deeper reflection and clarity.

Dream 1: I open a door in my office and discover a new room.
Restate the dream as a question: What new possibilities are opening up at work? In Life? Do I need to start an open door policy at work? Or in other areas of my life?

Dream 2: A huge tidal wave is bearing down on me. I run away, terrified.
Restate the dream as a question: What feelings do I allow to overwhelm me? What can I do to face my fears in a way that is supportive and healing?

In short:
What question or questions is the dream asking you? What question do you want to ask your dreams?

This method of inquiry into the meaning of a dream can be very enlightening. Below is a list of questions to consider in order to develop a greater understanding of what the subconscious is trying to reveal to you.

Inquiry

*A dream is a theater in which the dreamer
is himself the scene, the player,
the prompter, the producer, the author,
the public, and the critic.*

—Carl Jung, Psychological Reflections

- How are you, as dream ego, acting in this dream?
- What symbols in this dream are important to you?
- What are your actions?
- What is the helping or healing force?
- What is being wounded or healed?
- What would you like to avoid in the dream?
- What do you want to embrace?
- What actions might this dream suggest you consider in your waking life?
- What does this dream want from you?
- What situations seem unresolved?

- What seem resolved or complete?
- What other points of view beside your own can you find in the dream?

Rewording the previous questions may open up fresh paths of exploration to get to the heart of your unique 'Dream Speak'.

"Another technique to employ in your search for understanding is termed Dream Messaging. It involves sharing and comparing your findings with others."

Massaging Dreams in a Group of Two or More

I recommend finding others with whom to share your dreams.

I have a dream-sharing partner who lives out of state. Monthly, we discuss our dreams and our daily life. In so doing, we exchange insights, awarenesses, and feedback.

Here are a few guidelines:

- Dreams have multiple meanings and layers.
- Even when a dream meaning eludes you, it can still be helpful to sit with and hold the dream images. They appeared for a reason.

- Only the dreamer knows whether an interpretation is right for him or her. We cannot foist interpretations on to someone else.
- Symbols mean different things to all of us. A plane may mean freedom to me, and terror to someone afraid of flying.
- Most characters and images represent a part of us. Your dream of Aunt Pat may not be about Aunt Pat. Rather, it may be about the part of you that shares qualities you perceive in her.
- Trust your inner shifts or aha! feelings to determine whether you are on the right track or not.
- All dream group participants should discuss whether they want to maintain anonymity in all discussions of dream work outside of the group.
- When talking to others about their dreams, preface your remarks with, "If it were my dream…" No judgments are made. It is a collective brainstorm. Use kindness and show respect at all times.
- An Aha! moment is a reliable touchstone of successful dream work.

Dream analysis is a fruitful tool for understanding your state of mind. Use it if you wish to expand your personal awareness.

Suggested Reading:

Dreams and Spiritual Growth—A Judeo-Christian Way to Dreamwork including 37 Dreamwork techniques by Louis M. Savary, Patricia H. Berne, Stephan Kaplan Williams, Paulist Press.

Dreaming Myself, Dreaming a Town, by Sue Watkins. Watkins, the editor of a newspaper in a small town in New York, asked interested residents to record their dreams and send them to her. Once collected, she noticed, to her surprise, that people who did not know each other had similar dreams or dream images during the same week. Weeks before a fire broke out in town, residents reported fire images in their dreams, or dreams of feeling burnt out. What does that say about our collective consciousness? Are we communicating with each other via our dreams? What does that say about the nature of reality?

Dream Work: Techniques for Discovering the Creative Power in Dreams, by Jeremy Taylor.

Symbolically, the turtle's rounded shell represents heaven and its underbelly represents the earth slowly revolving

The Addiction Treatment Map

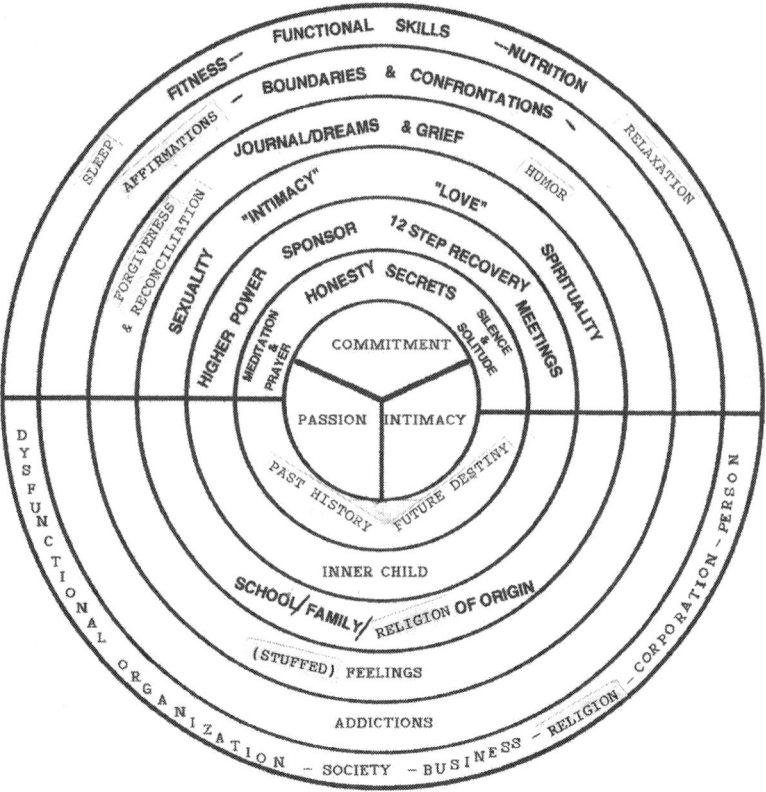

From the bottom to middle are the onion layers of why we get sick / addicted

The top to the middle of the circle are the layers of wellness, wholeness, and healing

Definition for the Center Circle:

INTIMACY: My being me and letting you see that. From the Latin "in timare" meaning "into my fears." Or "Into me I see."

PASSION: Excitement & Enthusiasm.

COMMITTMENT: Sustained choice over a specific period of time.

LOVE: Will to extend oneself for the purpose of nurturing one's own or another's spiritual growth. It is a daily decision.

SOLITUDE: Furnace of Transformation.

Map Descriptions of Feelings which are closest to the soul:

Excess	Feeling	Gift
Terror/Panic	Fear	Wisdom
Despair	Lonely	Reaching Out
Outrage	Anger	Energy
Unforgiveness	Guilt	Values
Worthlessness	Shame	Humility
Depression	Pain	Healing
Religiosity	Joy	Ecstasy

It's important we get in touch with our feelings and determine what baggage we are carrying from the past (EXCESS) and dump or eradicate it. That's when we'll experience and accept the corresponding GIFT(S). That explains in a nutshell the Therapeutic Healing Process. The left side will kill us and the right side will redeem and heal us. Basic Feeling acronym is (FLAGS PJ)

Chapter Five

Wholistic Health

*The secret of health for both mind and body
is not to mourn for the past, nor to worry
about the future, nor anticipate troubles
but to live the present moment
wisely and earnestly.*

—Buddha

During the years I worked with the church outside the Las Vegas Strip, I would travel on my day off to a cabin in the mountains as often as I could. Opening my eyes to birds and squirrels instead of neon signs, hearing the wind in the pine trees, smelling the silence, fed my soul. It felt like a soothing massage. Time stood still. Simplicity nourished me. I was present and felt the Presence. Now that is holistic health.

Many spiritual teachers talk about the necessity of living in the present moment. But who wants to be present in the midst of climate catastrophes? Political divisiveness? How can I even reach the present when my brain feels scrambled most of the time? It's simpler than you think. Because it's not about thinking. It's about being. You can't think your way into being or force yourself into being. It's a practice. Practicing being leads to well-being.

It's a paradox. The more physically present and open you are to your body, your emotions, one small moment at a time, the more peaceful and whole you become, no matter how turbulent the world is around you. It's like a stream or altered state of consciousness where I am one within and without.

"Most Americans (55%) recall feeling stressed much of the day in 2018," USA Today reported in April 2019.

"Even as their economy roared, more Americans were stressed, angry and worried last year than they have been at most points during the past decade," Julie Ray, a Gallup editor, wrote in a summary report.

Knowing this only reinforces my mission to share the tools that have helped me navigate my way through life challenges. As I stated in the Griefworks chapter, many people don't even realize they are harboring tremendous amounts of grief and trauma about things that happened years ago. The unacknowledged, unexpressed pain, only exacerbates any struggles they experience in the present.

I know. I am a sexual abuse survivor and a whistleblower. I know personally that Life, including my life in particular, is ever-evolving. My life is not permanently constricted or defined by my story. No one's is. Once you are present with your feelings, any addictions, emotional torment, physical symptoms, lessen their grip. It is never too late to enjoy a safe , serene and secure life. And that doesn't take a lot of money, either. It's a process. It takes reminding, reflecting, retrospective writing and reminiscing again and again.

When I met the highly stressed and agitated inmates I'd be working with at the federal prison, I was excited about sharing the abundance of simple tools I'd discovered. But my supervisors constantly thwarted or ignored my creative suggestions. No one encouraged me.

Eventually, I became depressed, which showed up as a throbbing pain right in the back of my neck. The throbbing pain led to migraines. I'd been stuffing my feelings of fear, frustration and anger for a long time. I knew that when you chronically stuff your feelings instead of feeling them and moving through them, they can express themselves in physical symptoms, minor at first, to get your attention. Then if you don't listen, they can manifest in disease. Dis-ease.

The warden and chaplain supervisor recognized my sadness and asked if I wanted to talk to a psychiatrist. I did. I told the gentleman, "This is what's happening. This is why and here's what I'm going to do about it." I would not take Zoloft, a synthetic anti-depressant. I would take St. John's Wort, an herbal supplement that also relieves depression. (Note: Do more research on St. John's Wort, if you are considering it for yourself or a loved one.) I would rent "I Love Lucy" and "The Three Stooges" and other shows and films that made me laugh. I would walk, swim, meditate, write in my journal, and eat sushi. Then I would focus on the positives—what I enjoyed and appreciated about my life, myself and the world, no matter how mundane or transcendent.

I didn't know it then, but I was using positive psychology, which accesses the power of awe, gratitude, love, amusement, compassion, contentment, joy and pride for the purpose of increased physical health and well-being.

There is a growing body of scientific evidence

to support the link between positive emotions and health. A University of California Berkeley study, published in the journal, "Emotion," in January 2019, suggests that feeling awe has an anti-inflammatory effect, protecting the body from chronic disease. It also enhances creative thinking and creates a sense of having enough time in the day.

No wonder I told my supervisor, "I think I'm getting better," when he called a few weeks later asking when I'd return. I felt lighter, freer. The pain in the neck vanished.

Within 6 weeks, I returned to work. After only two weeks back, my pain and depression returned. I knew I couldn't stay at my job any longer. Yes, I could take care of myself on the inner level. But I knew nothing would ever improve on the outer level. I was wasting my time, talent and treasure. I gave notice and eventually found a job at a mission where I was able to share the tools from my functioning toolkit.

How did I even become attracted to non-traditional approaches to body-mind health? Must have been another gift from my right brain. I dabbled in it until 1972. I was 30 years old. I felt healthy and strong. I picked up a child and suddenly my back locked up on me. I couldn't believe it. Friends hauled me to the hospital. The tests couldn't find anything wrong with me. But it woke me up and confirmed that I was not invincible. I needed regular exercise, nutrition, journaling, social interactions, dreams, mindfulness, living in the moment, and calming classical music. What works is different for every person. Consider or pause to write down what inspires well-being for you.

It was then that I realized I had to get serious. This could happen again. What was I doing wrong? What did I need to do positively on a regular basis? Since they couldn't uncover why this happened, I had to find my own answers. How was I to live my life without pain and agony? What about you? What gives your life meaning, serenity, peace?

I needed to use my tools with fortitude and ferocity. That would take discipline, motivation, organization--- all the things I list during a job interview. Executing that type of exploration and tenacity has given me strength, will power, and determination for the rest of my life.

Experiment & Questions

Recall a moment or time period when you felt vibrantly healthy. What was happening in your life? Where were you? How old? What kinds of relationships did you have? What kind of job did you have? Or hobby? What did you eat? What kinds of thoughts and emotions run through your system?

Let yourself explore. It may feel like you are imagining some answers. That's okay. Conjure up that feeling of health as vividly as possible. Feed that sense of aliveness and wellbeing in your body today. How can you stimulate your immune system?

Listen to your body. What does it need to boost more health? How can you nourish and sustain it? Jot down the answers or just marinate in that sensation. Or both. There is no right or wrong. There is only what is true for you.

Time Traveling Heals

The past and future are not inherently troublesome or something to be avoided. They can be used as tools in the NOW to help you become more alive in the Moment.

1. Dear Diary
Take a situation you want to change, a challenge you want to address, or something you've been longing to create, and write a letter to your diary as

if that change, solution, or creation has already happened and you can't wait to tell your diary about it. Add as much or as little detail as desired. Play, experiment. Notice the change in the sensations in your body and emotions as you experience what you want in the NOW.

2. Retrospective Writing

A mystic from New Mexico taught retrospective writing to my meditation group. Retrospective Writing is reimagining a pivotal negative moment in the past. I turn to retrospective writing when a moment from the past haunts me and I want to do something more than incubate a dream. It is not simply writing about an event or conjuring all your emotions from the past.

It is about Interrupting an agitated loop or trance of less than healthy thinking. With retrospective writing, I re-envision or re-enter a particular moment using my current wisdom to guide me. In this way, I eliminate the victim woe-is-me sadness. I rewrite the script so that it is more positive, joyful, hopeful.

Here is a real moment that previously caused me pain: In high school, on the first Sunday of the month, students were allowed visitors—family, friends. I never had visitors. No one brought me food because my family lived out of State. I'd watch, feeling increasingly jealous, angry and torn as other students picnicked with their families until 5 p.m., eating fried chicken or submarine sandwiches.

Here is how I transformed that painful moment through retrospective writing:

Every first Sunday of the month I hire food trucks. They park near the front of the school. Everybody is invited to enjoy a rotating selection of Chinese, Mexican, Mediterranean, Italian, Lebanese, German, or ice cream treats. Everyone celebrates this abundance of cultural, heritage, and historical cuisine. At the end of the day, we are all happy, satisfied, and well-fed.

Retrospective writing doesn't need to be novel-length. Here's another real life dilemma I felt called to resolve from that same time period: I desperately wanted to keep food in my room but there was no way to refrigerate it.

In my retro writing I imagine: In October, November, February, March, and April, I choose any kind of food I want from my dad's store. Then he ships it to me. I am excited, nurtured, nourished.

It may seem simple, but what I create through retrospective writing helps me in the present and gives the future hope. Through the writing, I realize more options exist than I imagine and I apply that knowing to my life now. Today I transform some of the food I receive with Meals on Wheels. For example, I get two hamburgers on Tuesdays. I don't gobble them both down. Instead I save one, make spaghetti sauce, and create a whole new meal.

Retro writings have helped me with my emotions about Amy's illnesses and her chemotherapy and radiation treatments. After Amy was diagnosed with cancer, I wasn't about to argue with the medical establishment. I've since discovered immunotherapy. I elaborate on what we can do to enhance her immune system and let her body heal.

By changing the scripts of any old story, I stop beating myself up. I feel an elation that releases my hurt, not just fleetingly, but forever. I solve it—whatever it happens to be.

Emotional Freedom Technique: a tool for clearing and cleansing your psyche without diving into your story

Spiritual Energy Transference—sending our energy to others sparks healing and jumpstarts their energy.

Bibliography

Calm Clarity: How to Use Science to Rewire Your Brain for Greater Wisdom, Fulfillment, and Joy, by Due Quach. Discover we have three brains: Reptilian, Teen Wolf, and Sage Brain. www.calmclarity.org Calm Clarity, Mindful Leadership Inclusion, & Unconscious Bias, USA.

Calm Clarity helps you and your organization maximize performance, enhance inclusion and diversity, and thrive in a rapidly changing 21st century environment. Our unique approach uses neuroscience and mindfulness to deconstruct unconscious bias, and foster genuine inclusion, engagement, leadership, and collaboration (www.calmclarity.org).

Anatomy of an Illness and Head First: The Biology of Hope and the Healing Power of Spirit, by Norman Cousins also by the same author *Laughter is the Best Medicine.*

Gesundheit: Good Health is a Laughing Matter, by Dr. Patch Adams and Maureen Mylander.

The Biology of Belief: Unleashing the Power of Consciousness, Matter & Miracles by Bruce H. Lipton, Ph.D.

Molecules Of Emotion: The Science Behind Mind-Body Medicine, by Candace B. Pert, Ph.D.

Chapter Six

Relationship is Life

*When love comes into your life,
unrecognized dimensions of your destiny
awaken and blossom and grow.*

—John O'Donohue

When I got married, that action caused me to lose my job. It all began while I was researching the origins of clerical celibacy in the university library. I fell in love with the librarian that assisted me. Her name was Amy. Three years later I became her husband.

Jung would have enjoyed this synchronicity, which he defined as a "meaningful coincidence" not explained by "conventional mechanisms of causality." Synchronicities possess a magical, inevitable feel in the realm of falling in love. Couples typically love to tell and retell the stories of how they met. They relive all the mysterious behind-the-scenes choreography that set them up to find each other at just the right time. Dismissing such moments as random coincidence is easy in more mundane areas of life. Synchronicities in love invite wonder. They imply a tangible sense that maybe Life, Divinity, or our Creator has a benevolent plan for us after all.

What is your love story? (If you are currently not in a relationship, let a previous one come to mind.) How did you meet? What synchronicities or chance encounters played a part in your meeting?

If you feel so inspired, wander through other areas of your life and recall one or two significant synchronicities. How do such moments affect your feelings about life and your relationship to it and to other people? How did it change, challenge, rearrange, thwart, or expand your life?

THE STORY OF MY SYNCHRONICITY

Apparently, our Creator wanted this priest and that librarian to meet. Although the attraction between Amy and I was instantaneous, our relationship evolved at a pace our hearts could handle. It was not so fast that the surprise of our connection overwhelmed us. And, it was not so slow that we couldn't take advantage of what we'd soon discover was our limited time together.

What about my ministry as a Catholic priest? Was I betraying my faith? No, I was not. Didn't this shake up my sense of self and the paradigm that supported it? Yes, and I was ready. I didn't know it then, but Life had been preparing me for this spectacular leap.

Years earlier, at the age of 41, I had fallen in love for the first time. It was an ecstatic and excruciatingly painful experience. As a Catholic priest, of course, I was not allowed to acknowledge my simple human need to be vulnerable with someone special to me. I was not allowed to revel in another's presence or enjoy shared sexuality. Although I was lonely and dazzled by her brilliance, I could not let it evolve. It took me years to grieve that unfulfilled love.

While I was grieving, I also longed for a loving foundation and support system. As the only unmarried chaplain working at a federal prison, I got stuck covering for everyone else. I worked while the other chaplains vacationed with their wives or took care of them when they were sick. I did not have a loved one to travel with or nurture. It felt lopsided;

increasingly unfair. I wanted what they had. I struggled with a growing sense of loneliness. Now, I am grateful for that longing and loneliness. They were calls from my Spirit for a larger, more authentic life.

At about this time, as I have mentioned previously, I decided to do some research on clerical celibacy. I soon discovered that at the beginning of Christianity, priests were allowed to marry. Then, I learned that in the 12th century, the Church hierarchy consciously decided to change the marital rules for clerics. They banned priestly marriage and mandated clerical celibacy. The undeclared motivation for this decision was two-fold. First, this action provided enhanced control over the priests. Second, it also eliminated the obligation to provide for the needs of priestly dependents. As a result, the Church would soon amass greater wealth.

With this revelatory information, an inner light turned on for me. With it came a rush of relief and acceptance. I felt the grandeur of God fully alive! I was in love. Someone loved me back. Amy and I talked easily about everything. As a child, she had asked a lot of questions of the Sunday school teachers and priests at her Catholic Church. "Because I said so," they responded. That wasn't good enough for Amy. At the age of 16, she dumped Catholicism.

After 31 years of working on its behalf, the Church left me as well. Amy and I became husband and wife in 1999. I was removed from the priesthood and thereby lost my job.

Know Thyself & Pay Attention

Preparation is Essential for a Successful Marriage.

At last I felt whole and congruent. My inner life matched my outer one. As John O'Donohue says, "Real friendship or love is not manufactured or achieved by an act of will or intention. Friendship is always an act of recognition." Just because Amy and I recognized each other and felt a synergy didn't mean we were prepared for the daily ins and outs of an intimate relationship.

Who is prepared? How many of us have any formal Relationship 101 training? Preparation is key to all vocations. Whether you're a doctor, contractor, lawyer, plumber or beautician, you are required to have some schooling, preparation or on-the-job training. In the military, your limitations and strengths are evaluated. To receive a driver's license, you are required to read a handbook, take a written test, and pass a driving and an eye test. Only then, do you obtain a driver's license. Moreover, the license is active for a specific time period. You need to renew it after so many years and you are required to obtain an auto license and insurance.

The only license that requires no training in any state is a marriage license. Typically, all a couple needs to do to get a marriage license is pay a fee. The state presumes that the couple already has at their disposal all the other capabilities necessary to create an enduring relationship.

But do they? Two people, no matter who they are or how miraculous their meeting, resonate for reasons that they usually do not consciously understand. Yes, Life may conspire forcing them to relate, but why?

As one marriage counselor said, "We become one parent and marry another." Is that true? Or is it true that we are attracted to someone who is our opposite so that we can work out unresolved issues from our past? Whatever our theories may be, most of us don't have the background, training, or resources necessary to build a loving and sustainable long-term relationship.

Moreover, I ask: how many of us are trained in the non-romantic practical aspects of living with someone else? As a priest, I had a head start. One of my duties was to facilitate marriage and relationship preparation courses. At the time, I wondered how could I possibly give a marriage preparation course without being married myself. I eagerly sought and accepted wisdom from married couples, counselors, and authors of books on relationships. I had no idea that one day I would benefit from all these practices I shared with other couples.

In that search for wisdom, I discovered the St. Mary's Press booklet entitled, *Perspectives on Marriage*. It contained tear-out pages that could be shared. The booklet guided couples to talk about communication, conflict resolution, their families of origin, hopes and dreams, intimacy, explosive issues, religious faith, money matters, spiritual values, and their wishes for planning a family. It is essential to explore these rarely discussed topics with compassion, intuition, and patience. If not done so, communication breaks down irrevocably. I found that the explorations in this booklet have the potential to inspire any couple to deepen their sense of intimacy, no matter what topic they explore. It is open to all faiths or no faith in English and Spanish.

The term intimacy comes from the Latin word intimare—"into my fears." It implies a desire to find somebody special that I can trust to share my fears with and who can share their fears with me. To expand upon this concept, intimacy can be rephrased as "Into me I see". It is about me looking into my own emotions and behavior. It is about understanding the why, what, where, and how of myself. It reveals the map of me. "My being me and letting you see that" is about knowing myself well enough to be transparent to my loved one, warts and all. It is also inextricably predicated upon trust.

I strongly recommend the reading of the Perspectives on Marriage booklet to anyone contemplating a relationship (see page 98).

My Personal Experience with Marital Intimacy

A month after Amy and I married, she was diagnosed with breast cancer. That propelled us to learn how to communicate every day on a deep feeling level. Initially, Amy wondered why I didn't intuit her feelings and thoughts. So, I began paying attention to her nonverbal communication. I looked for visual cues, voice intonations, and facial expressions.

We committed to living a conscious life together, affirming each other, compromising, and celebrating each other's dreams as much as we could. We realized that we were both blind as bats in certain areas of our perceptions. Without assistance, we could bump into lots of terrifying situations. To prevent this from happening, we sought outside help from social workers, counselors, workshops and happily married couples.

One recommendation that we received to enhance our mutual awareness was that we attend a **Marriage Encounter** program. In this guided program, couples are asked to engage in various tasks designed to enhance communication and intimacy between them. The process is divided into exercises carried out over the course of a weekend. The exercises are simple yet powerful, if fully embraced by both spouses. We both reflect on various marital questions. We write our personal responses and share that revelation exclusively with our mate. The overall experience was transformative, worthwhile and redemptive. We learned how to communicate effectively, quickly, and creatively.

After the Weekend, the process went something like this. First, we mutually picked questions about something meaningful and impactful in our relationship. There is a whole list of questions provided.

In our case, we chose "How do I feel about you having cancer? How do I feel about having cancer?"

How do I feel about being your caregiver? How do I feel about receiving care? What are your feelings about our budget? What are your feelings about our sexual relationship?

We each wrote about our feelings in vivid detail. Then, we took turns sharing what we wrote with each other reading once with the head and once with the heart.

We didn't judge, ask questions, problem solve, or give advice. This wasn't about fixing anything. This was about developing the capacity to share feelings and truly listen.

As Mark Nepo, the healing arts teacher, says, "To listen is to lean in, softly, with a willingness to be changed by what we hear."

Every time Amy and I shared in this way, we felt infinitely closer. From that closeness, it was easy for us to make choices and decisions as a union.

As a consequence of this shared experience, I now consider a relationship or a marriage as being a process. It is not a static container comprised of two people. Rather, it is a journey shared by two people wherein they gently and lovingly rub off each other's rough edges so that each person becomes more loving, realistic and compassionate. If that happens, as it did with us, we are thankful and grateful.

How to Enhance Intimacy in Relationships

To explore and enhance your own sense of intimacy, reflect and answer the following questions together:

- What are you most thankful about in our relationship?
- What inspires you to connect more deeply with your partner?
- Describe an act of bravery involving Love.
- If you could give your younger self some tips on sustaining a loving relationship with someone, what would they be?
- What actions could I take to enhance the intimacy between me and my loved one? What lessons or stories will I share with my progeny?

Resources for Further Reading, Reflections, or Googling

Perspectives on Marriage, (St. Mary's Press (800) 533-8095, 702 Terrace Heights, Winona, MN 85987. This is excellent for preparing for any relationship. $10 plus shipping. English, Spanish or Ecumenical

Enneagram: Nine Sufi Points of Compulsions and the Connections of Personalities. Google it. *The Enneagram* by Helen Palmer.

Myers-Briggs Test: A personality inventory of how opposites connect. Google it. *Please Understand Me: An Essay on Temperament Styles,* by David Kersey and Marilyn Bates.

AFFIRMATIONS

I am free to be me
I am free to grow in my own inner light
I love myself unconditionally
I am a perfect expression of God's love
I am willing to succeed
I am peaceful and loving
I am powerful
I am willing to love and be loved
I now feel love connected to my parents
I am generous and caring
I am patient and kind
I feel creative and I am creative
I solve situations creatively
I deserve to be rich
I have incredible self-confidence
Every day in every way I get better
      and better and better
I share my love with myself and others
I give and accept unconditional love
I now allow myself to be loved
      and supported by others
I am a radiant human being

AFFIRMATIONS

I love life and life loves me
I am now good to myself
I achieve all my goals
Money works for me
I draw great things to me
Endless good comes to me in endless ways
I am healthy, happy and full of life
I am enthusiastic, motivated and focused
I do what I need to do with joy and delight
My mind is unlimited in its power to assist me
I can do it! I KNOW I can do it
I now make the decision to accomplish my goals
I can do anything I decide to do
I have the power and the ability to do whatever I want to do
I know exactly what I want, I focus my energy upon my goal
I have the energy, concentration and determination to do it
I go for it
I accept myself unconditionally, and I am worthy of love

Chapter Seven
Discoveries Along My Mississippi Cruise

In September, 2019, I took a 14-day cruise down the Mississippi on the newly built riverboat named "American Harmony" to witness the climate crisis emergency currently unfolding in Middle America. Spring weather that year brought incredible flooding to the North, leaching pesticides, herbicides and fertilizers into rivers. This flow stimulated the growth of toxic blue-green algae which caused the closing of all the Mississippi State beaches, and created a Dead Zone in the Gulf of Mexico.

The Upper Mississippi was created by glaciers millions of years ago. Since that time, many dams and locks have been added to control the flow of the river.

During my trip down the Mississippi, I interviewed real estate agents, financial advisors, local elders, Native Americans, Blacks, Hispanics and tourism officials. I asked them about empty storefronts, the local culture, history, customs, and weather patterns. I observed the changes in land environment may cause severe disruptions to finances, migration, bigotry, racism, ethics, morals and values.

Native Americans made treaties in an attempt to preserve their land but most of these agreements were broken by the American Government. It is a tragic story of greed, mistrust, and genocide still perpetuated today.

St. Louis southward is smooth sailing on the Mississippi. This section is full of Civil War sights and memories. During the passage through this area, informative historical lectures were given on board by the great, great, great grandson of Jefferson Davis, the first President of the Confederacy. It was informative, interesting and sometimes biased.

As my journey continued, I observed more empty storefronts, churches and banks but with few people around. I learned that most folks now shop at Walmart or online at Amazon. Hence, the town centers are becoming blighted.

This trip, ending in New Orleans, confirmed for me the why, what, where, when and how of the global climate catastrophe. It is manifested by the pestilence, fierce frequent hurricanes, the Heartland floods, the horrendous raging California forest fires, the Venice, Italy flooding, and the vanishing ice in Greenland, the Arctic and the Antarctic. Everything is connected and climate scientists agree.

I now understand and appreciate the connections between the original Joan of Arc and the modern-day Joan of Arc, Greta Thunberg. Both were 16 years old when they began their quest. The alarm that they raised can be summarized in five words: "Our House is on Fire!"

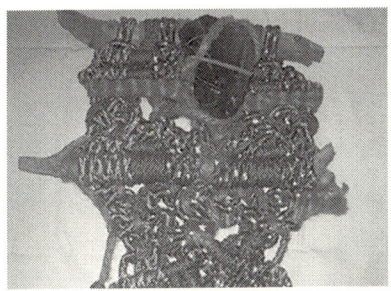

As I do on all my journeys, I created a Mississippi macramé hanging composed of dried driftwood with a red heart shaped obsidian stone at the top. I used bright green, brown, red, and silver cords fashioned from the concept in my right brain symbolizing various sights, sounds, and memories.

At St. Louis, I discovered and added another abandoned hanging limb. I did this so the macramé would also represent my journey southward past Memphis, Vicksburg, Baton Rouge, New Orleans and onward to the Dead Zone in the Gulf of Mexico.

Hope and Tragedy, Suffering and Success, Darkness and Light

Whenever I addressed the climate crisis with others along the journey, I was asked if I was an "activist" or "environmentalist?" "No," I replied, "I am just an inquisitive observer of people, nature, and situations."

Evading or denying the fearful realities of impending doom and gloom is counterproductive to survival. Equally damaging is any tactic designed to shoot the messenger.

My journey's pervading purpose was to see the American Heartland with all its history, customs, culture, heritage, and memories in the light of the tragic toxic climate crisis mirrored throughout the planet.

"Our House is indeed on Fire!" as Greta states, "You are robbing me of my future existence!"

Throughout this book I have endeavored and suggested various tips, tools, techniques, maps, and aides for inner and outer serenity. They offer peace despite the climate crisis and the global pandemic virus.

It is unnecessary to perpetuate past mistakes. We can solve the climate crisis and Pandemic deaths, if we act individually, collectively and in concert with world governments. In so acting, we will restore peace, harmony, and health to ourselves and renewed vigor to our Planet.

The Global Pandemic

Regarding the American Covid-19, we have two groups of people: The **Careful**—who follow laws, protocols, masks, self-distancing, with hand washing and the **Careless**—who appear selfish, stubborn, greedy, spoilt, sluggish, mistrusting, entitled, "my way is the only way," and "it is a free county so my wishes concern no one else" attitude.

So, that is why most other Countries have met,

struggled, and defeated the virus while the USA continues with 1,000 daily deaths with no end in sight! There are sad, mad, and bad consequences for this behavior. Again, **"Our Nation is on Fire! Our Planet is on Fire!"**

I am neither a dualist nor a tribalist. I am a protagonist and an optimist. My lifelong motto is: **"To comfort the disturbed and to disturb the comfortable."**

Between the **Egg** and the **Ash,** what do we do with the **Dash?**

To be continued . . .

OTHER RESOURCES

How to Discover Your Personal Power and Connect to Collective Positive Opportunities and Potentials

Check Out These Resources:

- Library System: Books, Internet, Magazines, DVDs, Videos, Languages, Newspapers www.library…(choose your library) click on "Databases & Online Collections"

- Parks & Recreation: Catalog of Aquatics, Swimming, Walking, Dancing, Hobbies, Painting, Art, Creating, Sports, Writing, Journalingt, Dreaming, Gym, Yoga, Card Games, Billiards, Tennis

- Community College: Catalog of Classes

- City Weekly: Sections on Special Events, Bulletin Board, Films, Gardening, Outdoors, Sports, Well-Being, Dance, Music, Theater, Art, Museums, Chow Scan

- Support Groups: Grief, Al-Anon, 12-Step Meetings. Gather your own Retired Old Men/Ladies Eating Out groups (ROMEO/ROLEO)

- Alternative Healing Options: Tai Chi, Chi Qigong, Reiki, Massage, Acupuncture,

Meditation, Chanting, Singing, Music, Healing Touch, Yoga, Laughing Yoga

- Spiritual Consciousness: On inernet at: refdesk.com, google.com, beliefnet.com. Nature hikes, listen to silence and solitude. 62+ Golden Eagle Pass for free entrance to all national parks ($10.00)

"Not what we believe, but what we positively practice."

"Visualize positive outcomes with intentions, affirmations, and attractions."

"I am me, perfect in every way, living my bliss today and letting go of past and future while embracing the present NOW without resentment nor resistance but with forgiveness, love, and service."

"I expect prosperity, abundance, wealth, health, happiness, spirituality, authenticity, honesty and _____."

List your **OWN** resources here:

Co-Dependency is: A pattern of painful dependency on compulsive behaviors and on approval from others in an attempt to find safety, self worth, and identity. Recovery is possible.

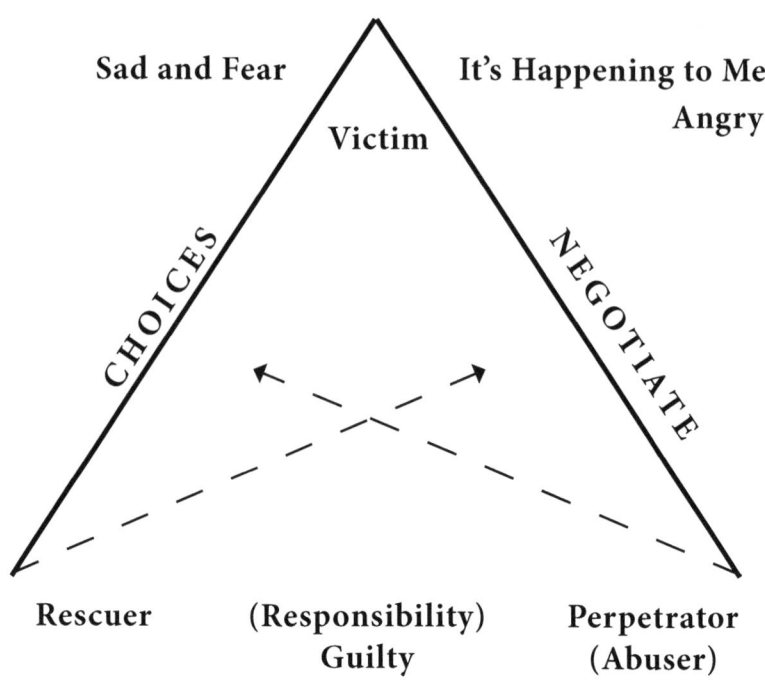

Sad and Fear — Victim — It's Happening to Me / Angry

CHOICES — NEGOTIATE

Rescuer — (Responsibility) Guilty — Perpetrator (Abuser)

Rescuer	Perpetrator
enabling, caretaking, fixing, people pleasing, denying, super _____, tolerating, keeping secrets, not confronting, buying gifts, not setting boundaries, eating, drinking, sex, eliminating consequences, etc.	emotional, mental, physical, spiritual, criticize, tease, humiliate, withdraw, being late, sarcasm, cynicism, eyebrow raising, tsking, sighing, drinking, eating, affairs, spending, self-righteous, patronizing, suicide, over exercise, illness, negative self talk, blame, etc.

Interrupting Bias: Calling Out vs. Calling In

Calling Out:

- When we need to let someone know that their words or actions will not be tolerated.
- When we need to interrupt in order to prevent further harm
- Will likely feel hard and uncomfortable, but necessary
- Allows us to hit the "pause" button and break the momomentum

Wow. Nope. Ouch. I need to stop you right there.	That word/comment is really triggering and offensive. Be mindful and pick a different word.	I need to push back against that. I disagree. I don't see it that way.
Okay, I'm having a strong reaction to that & I need to let you know why.	I don't find that funny. Tell me why that's funny to you.	I wonder if you've considered the impact of your words.
Hmm, maybe you want to think this one through a bit more and talk about it later	I need you to know how your comment just landed on me.	That's not our culture here. Those aren't our values.

Calling Out (Continued):

Are the following relevant to your point? How? Sex, gender, gender identity, gender expression, race, class, religion, age, immigration status, body type, marital status, pregnancy?	It sounded like you just said: _____. Is that really what you meant?	I feel obligated as your peer/colleague/friend/co-worker/supervisor to tell you that your comment wasn't okay.
It sounds like you're making some assumptions that we need to unpack a bit.	You may or may not realize this, but you're talking about me/my story/my identity markers.	I need to leave the room if ther conversation is going to continue down this road.

Remember: it is a powerful thing for the target of oppression to hear these words from the mouth of an ally!

Calling In:

- When there's an opportunity to explore deeper, make meaning together, and find a mutual sense of understanding across difference
- When we're seeking to understand or learn more
- When we want to help imagine different perspectives, possibilities, or outcomes
- Provides for multiple perspectives and encourages paradigm shifts
- Focused on reflection, not reaction

- Is *not* just a suggestion with an uptick (Don't you think you should...?)

I'm curious; what was your intention when you said that?	How might the impact of your words/actions differ from your intent?	What sort of impact do you think your decision/comment/action might have?
How might someone else see this differently? Is it possible that someone might misinterpret your words/actions?	How might your own comfort level, assumptions, expectations, prior experiences be influencing your beliefs, decisions, process?	How is _____ different from _____? What is the connection between _____ and _____?
What criteria are you using to measure/assess etc?	How did you decide, determine, conclude...	What would have to change in order for _____?
What do you assume to be true about _____?	Why is this the best way to proceed? What other approaches have you considered?	What is making you the most fearful, nervous, uncomfortable, or worried?
Why do you think that is the case? Why do you believe that to be true?	Why do you think others have or have not moved in that direction?	How do you know it's working?
Why did the result or response cause a problem for you?	What would other stakeholders say/think/feel?	In your opinion, what is the best case scenario?

Think: How might we call out the behavior, while calling in the person?

I read of a man who stood to speak at the funeral
of a friend. He referred to the dates on his
tombstone from the beginning to the end.

The Dash

He noted that first came his date of birth
and spoke the following date with tears,
but said what mattered most of all
was the dash between those years.

For that dash represents all the time
that they spent alive on the earth . . .
and now only those who love him
know what that little line is worth.

For it matters not, how much we own;
the cars . . . the house . . . the cash,
what matters is how we live and love,
and how we spend our dash.

So think about this long and hard . . .
Are there things you'd like to change?
For you never know how much time is left,
that can still be rearranged.

If we could just slow down enough
to consider what's true and real,
and always try to understand
the way other people feel.

And be less quick to anger,
and show appreciation more,
and love the people in our lives
like we've never loved before.

If we treat each other with respect,
and more often wear a smile . . .
remembering that this special dash
might only last a little while.

So, when your eulogy's being read
with your life's actions to rehash . . .
would you be proud of the things they say
about how you spent your dash?

Made in the USA
Monee, IL
26 November 2020

49679620R00072